Draeger

Pioneering Leader in Asian Martial Traditions

An Anthology of Articles from the *Journal of Asian Martial Arts*
Compiled by Michael A. DeMarco, M.A.

Disclaimer
Please note that the authors and publisher of this book are not responsible in any manner whatsoever for any injury that may result from practicing the techniques and/or following the instructions given within. Since the physical activities described herein may be too strenuous in nature for some readers to engage in safely, it is essential that a physician be consulted prior to training.

All Rights Reserved
No part of this publication, including illustrations, may be reproduced or utilized in any form or by any means, electronic or mechanical, including photocopying, recording, or by any information storage and retrieval system (beyond that copying permitted by sections 107 and 108 of the US Copyright Law and except by reviewers for the public press), without written permission from Via Media Publishing Company.

Warning: Any unauthorized act in relation to a copyright work may result in both a civil claim for damages and criminal prosecution.

Copyright © 2016 by
Via Media Publishing Company
941 Calle Mejia #822
Santa Fe, NM 87501 USA
E-mail: md@goviamedia.com

All articles in this anthology were originally
published in the *Journal of Asian Martial Arts*.
Listed according to the table of contents for this anthology:

Smith, R. (1999), Vol. 8, No. 3, pp. 18-33
Draeger, D. (1999), Vol. 8, No. 3, pp. 34-37
Davey, H. (1996), Vol. 5 No. 1, pp. 96-103
Friman, H. (1999), Vol. 8 No. 3, pp. 38-41

Book and cover design by Via Media Publishing Company
Edited by Michael A. DeMarco, M.A.

Cover illustration
Artwork by Michael Lane.
www.golfandsportsbylane.com ©1999

ISBN: 978-1893765313

contents

iv **Preface**
   by Michael DeMarco, M.A.

CHAPTERS

1 **Donn F. Draeger: A Lifelong Embodiment of the Samurai Code**
   by Robert W. Smith, M.A.

21 **Letters on Miyamoto Musashi**
   by Donn F. Draeger

25 **Donn Draeger and the International Hoplology Society**
   by Hugh E. Davey

34 **Donald F. Draeger's Wisconsin Grave**
   by H. Richard Friman, Ph.D.

38 **Index**

preface

Donn Draeger was the most influential martial artist/scholar of the 20th century. His more than twenty books and long list of accomplishments support this argument. For this reason, we are publishing this anthology of articles that focus on this outstanding person. Although short in length, this book is rich in content covering the inspiring life and contributions of a leading pioneer in the Asian martial traditions.

The author of the first chapter, Robert W. Smith, was a close confidant of Draeger during his career. With Draeger, Smith co-authored the classic *Asian Fighting Arts* (later renamed as *Comprehensive Asian Fighting Arts*). Smith was in a unique position to provide details about Draeger's character, academic and martial skills.

Donn Draeger wrote two letters to Smith (dated September 2, 1969 and June 29, 1981) that gave insight into Miyamoto Musashi. Smith was writing a book review and asked Draeger for his opinion on the historical swordsman. With the help of Joseph Svinth, Smith merged and edited these letters. This contains Draeger's response in his typically ebullient tone of correspondence with Smith.

Donn Draeger can easily be considered as the "father of Asian martial arts research" in the West since he conducted pioneering research in the field and was one of the highest ranking black belts in a number of Japanese combative arts. As a scholar, he became involved in a Japanese research society for martial arts, and built upon it. Author Hugh Davey writes on the founding and influence of the International Hoplology Society Draeger founded.

Draeger shaped the lives of several generations of martial artists. It was unknown to most that he had died in a Wisconsin hospital following medical treatments for natural sicknesses and perhaps for poisoning. In the last chapter, Dr. Friman tells of his discovery of Donn Draeger's gravesite. Finding his grave in 1998 brought proper respects from friends, including Kaminoda Tsunemori, master of jo and sword.

Scholars of combative traditions and martial arts practioners—especially those participating in the Japanese arts—will benefit greatly by reading this short anthology. Draeger's life is inspiring to both the scholar and practitioner.

Michael A. DeMarco, Publisher
Santa Fe, New Mexico
August 2016

— 1 —

Donn F. Draeger: A Lifelong Embodiment of the Samurai Code
by Robert W. Smith, M.A.

Looks like a kind going on an adventure.
Photo from the D.F. Draeger Archives.

Donn Draeger I have long regarded as one of the great samurai of the last half of the twentieth century. He was:

- The first and only non-Japanese to hold the rank of *budo kyoshi*, or full professor of the classical martial arts and ways.
- The first non-Japanese judo instructor at the Kodokan in Tokyo.
- The first non-Japanese to compete in the "All Japan High Rank Holders" judo tournament at the Kodokan.
- The creator of the recognized academic discipline of hoplology (the study of weapons and fighting systems). He also established the International Hoplological Research Center and published its newsletter.
- The creator of the U.S. Jodo Federation. (The *jo* is a Japanese short staff used as a weapon.)
- Almost solely responsible for uniting the various American judo organizations into the United States Judo Black Belt Federation.
- The person most responsible for introducing systematic weight training into Japanese competitive judo.
- The author of more than twenty books on the martial arts and ways.

I could go on and on: there was no end to the man. Sir Richard Francis Burton described a college friend who had passed away: "He was a good hand with his sword, always ready to fight, and equally ready to write." These words catch Donn as well.

I met Donn in 1948 or 1949. Johnny Osako of the Chicago Judo Club passed the word that a Marine captain back from the Pacific "holding a high judo rank" was coming to visit. The next afternoon a few of us were working out when in waltzed this big beautiful lug who looked like Randolph Scott's bigger brother and wore a uniform that had never been worn better, not even by John Wayne, in films. And this is not just memory talking. Donald Richie, a respected authority on Japanese culture, met Donn once in Tokyo. Afterward Richie said that Donn looked like a cross between Paul Newman and Mike Mazurki, the actor who played Moose Malloy ("You want I should bust this guy?") in *Murder My Sweet*, the fine film made from Raymond Chandler's *Farewell My Lovely* (1940).

The towering Donn Draeger.

The big one paused at the entrance, looked at us as if we were side dishes he hadn't ordered, and announced himself: "Donn Draeger, yodan." This was done with a panache I took for immodesty. I glanced at Johnny Osako who played it pianissimo, and then at Art Broadbent who arched an eyebrow before I could arch mine. After chatting for a half hour, Donn left, promising to return that evening.

Also, Art and I had tickets for a Russian language film of M.P. Mussorgsky's opera *Boris Godunov*. (I was deep into Russian then.) So we missed the massacre. Back from messing with tough Japanese and Korean judoka, Donn probably expected easy pickings from our midwestern hicks. Instead, he was turned every way but loose by Osako and colleagues. It was a hot time in the old town that night, and the pie poor Donn was made to eat was indeed humble.

After this, Donn returned to his hometown of Milwaukee and later opened the Detroit Judo Club. The latter had a wonderful sign on the front door reading, "Open 24 hours a day, 7 days a week." Sometime later, Donn moved to the Washington, DC area. After Donn's death, the owner of the first large weight-lifting gym there told me that Donn had been an avid iron pill pusher. He added that in 1950, the area big shots, possibly including Bob Hoffman, the owner of *Strength and Health* magazine at York, Pennsylvania—Donn was chums with him for years—wanted to promote Donn as a surething in that year's Mr. America contest. Donn refused, however, saying that he wanted to continue full-bore on judo. And that he did, establishing administrative procedures, organizing the United States into several regional black belt associations, starting a small magazine, and so on.

When wife Alice and I moved to the Washington, DC area in 1955, Donn was there to help us move in and get settled. For a year or so we were thick as thieves, practicing (a 1st-dan watching Donn and me randori at the Pentagon Dojo pronounced it the most stylish he'd ever seen—Donn made anyone look good), talking (about how the national judo effort should be organized), and scheming about future books we'd do. All too swiftly he was gone.

Left: Draeger receiving some lessons in judo from Ishikawa Takehiko (in 1984, at the age of 67, Ishikawa became the youngest 9th-dan in Kodokan history). **Right:** Ishkawa tosses Donn with a "sweeping loin" then places him in a cross armlock. *Photos courtesy of R. Smith.*

In 1956, on his last night in America before going to Japan, Donn and I had cheeseburgers in a small cafe near the old brewery on 26th Street in Washington. At the time, CIA was still using World War II temporary structures as offices, and famed Kodokan 6th-dan Pat O'Neill was teaching his brand of rough-and-tumble to Government personnel at the brewery and at the Marine Corps base at Quantico. That night, I recall playing Jimmy Dorsey's great number "So Rare" on the juke box and talking with Donn for hours. Other than leading a 1970 visit by a top-drawer Japanese weapons group (it starred T. Shimizu and T. Kaminoda), this was Donn's last day on the mainland before returning home to die in Wisconsin on October 21, 1982.

Other than the amount of time we spent in the States, Donn and I were alike in many respects. We probably felt the essence of the Asian martial arts more and earlier than most exponents in the West. We abhorred commercialism. And we liked to read and write. Early on, the leading American martial arts magazine offered us its editorial slot but when we insisted that it be substantively sound and non-commercial, and that it be changed from a monthly to a quarterly format to retain quality, the owner lost interest in us.

We had two movie nibbles. On one, I read the existing screenplay that had a finale of two disembodied swords fighting each other, and pronounced anathema on it. Directed by John Frankenheimer, *The Challenge* was released in 1982 without the sword denouement. The other, a documentary, died when we insisted on quality and time. They told a lot of lies before disappearing to look for money elsewhere.

But we never did do our journal. During the 1970s Donn put out several issues of *Martial Arts International* (MAI). While a good beginning, unfortunately, financial and other problems prevented it maturing into an institution. He asked me repeatedly for contributions, but my work, teaching, and family didn't give me the elbow room to help as much as I should have. I regret that now.

In Japan, Donn lived in a rambling house in the Ichigaya section of Tokyo. Big and well made, it nevertheless shivered its timbers when Wang Shuchin, the neijia master, would visit and punch anything anchored. By the time of my six-week stay in 1961, Wang had taken the best that several high-ranking Japanese karate, kempo, and other martial art experts could offer, and destroyed the indestructible Jon Bluming with a no-inch punch that the film actor Bruce Lee would have envied. Bluming tried to get even by taking a free hit at Wang's paunch and only hurt his own wrist. In Wang's taiji classes (he would not teach his forte, xingyi, to the Japanese then, but did later), he had many highly placed Japanese executives and a handful of *yakuza* (Mafia-style lowlifers). When other warriors of the night stalked him for a short time (Wang himself probably never knew this), one of his yakuza godfathers got wind of it, Donn told me, and the stalkers disappeared into the night mists.

Donn Draeger teaching the iron pill to All-Japan Judo Champion I. Inokuma (r) and Jon Bluming (l). *Photo from the D.F. Draeger Archives.*

While studying for my 3rd-dan in judo, I spent six weeks living in that storied house. Besides Donn, other residents included the aforementioned Jon Bluming, young Jim Bregman (the 1964 Tokyo Olympics third place winner), Doug Rogers (the Canadian heavyweight champion and a 2nd-place winner in the same Olympics), Bill Fuller, and a dyspeptic Japanese housekeeper with an expression stronger than Wang's punch. Her stony aspect was probably the result of the practical jokes this crew played. On anyone. I awoke my first morning there to find Donn holding a shinai one inch from my nose. Five minutes later I was killed again. As I was returning down the hall from the toilet to my room, Bluming and Fuller fell on me from opposite rooms with bo and kiai. Alertness was all—no one could afford to completely relax in that house. The occasional prank involving girlfriends and water-filled condoms often breached taste and brought a guarded tension to the occupants. As far as I know, it never went beyond that. Nor could it afford to. With those heavy hitters, a punch-out would have severely tested the house that had survived earthquakes, the massive firestorms created by US bombing in 1945, and Wang's occasional beatings since then.

Jimmy Bregman was the youngest in that house. I had known him in the Washington, DC area since he was fifteen when he tossed me with a shoulder throw to the merriment of Donn and others. He more than fulfilled his early promise by going off to Tokyo and placing third in the 1964 Olympics. Later he returned to America and a lot of the contest promise died when a freakish accident on the mat injured his leg. At lunch in Washington one day, he recalled what I'd told him about his training at the Kodokan in 1961. I had called it, he said, the judo gray life: "Every day you came to practice in drab surroundings, the air almost astringent with sweat. You doffed your street clothes and winced as you tried to get into your limpid heavy judogi, which never completely dried out from the exertions of the day before. You walked toward the mat and there first up for some rousing randori was the monster you were happy not to see the day before."

I knew Donn well before that time in his house in Tokyo, but there I got to see him up closer. I came to admire not only his high skills, but also how gladly and patiently he assisted foreigners with their problems. It was said that he had more than a hundred black belts in the various martial arts. While that may have been true, it seems excessive. But perhaps not. Douglas Chadwick said in his seminal *The Fate of the Elephant* (1992), "I wouldn't claim that all elephant stories are true—but with elephants, you don't need to make up all that much."

Donn Draeger, a sword and a kiai from a master of the Tenshin Shoden Katori Shito-ryu. Draeger performs the iaijutsu of the style. Photo taken in Malaysia in the mid-1970's. *Photo courtesy of the Jodo Federation of Malaysia.*

Master Otake Risuke of the ancient Katori Shinto-ryu.
Photo courtesy of P. Lineberger.

What I do know is this. In judo when his knees gave out, Donn pursued groundwork. I learned from a good source that he was in the top echelon in Japan in that area. I also learned that Donn taught a few top Japanese swordsmen in a mountain retreat for several weeks each year. As for details, I was never able to corroborate these claims because of the bureaucracy surrounding such things in Japan. But the fact that Isao Inokuma, who won the 1964 heavyweight judo title, told Japanese television journalists that Donn's coaching was the key to his success—an unprecedented acknowledgment by a Japanese judoka—gives one pause.

Donn and the Ichigaya gang were on call for film producers in Tokyo who needed foreign extras. Big Doug Rogers told me he had been every type of foreign soldier in battle scenes. Donn's most lucrative film work was for the James Bond series. In *You Only Live Twice* (1967), Donn was a stunt double for an out-of-shape, obviously bored Sean Connery. Of the movie, Paul Nurse commented, "Hollywood trashes budo again!"

Out on the bustling Tokyo streets we would walk, talk, and watch. There were the pipe dreams that never come to fruition. Donn was forever urging me to join his weapons safari in Malaysia. Later we were to edit a real martial arts journal. Still later I was to join him on the faculty at the University of Hawaii. These things never happened because our paths diverged. But we did do a book together—this was *Asian Fighting Arts* (1969), later retitled *Comprehensive Asian Fighting Arts* (1980).

Photo courtesy of the Jodo Federation of Malaysia.

He wrote a lot, too, even more than me. In all, Donn wrote more than thirty books. He pecked away at his small typewriter hours a day, instructing, clarifying, leading. His books were authentic, blending tradition and innovation. Though his prose was centered and vital, his inherent humor was absent.

Outside his books, which had all the wit and humor of Marine Corps administrative memoranda, Donn was always full of fun. I jumped him once for eating on the run. C.W. Nicol, in his excellent *Moving Zen: Karate as a Way to Gentleness* (1982), hits the same subject. Fourth dan karate sensei K. Enoeda grabbed a foreigner eating a banana in the dojo by the neck and set him down at a table. "You sit!" Enoeda was learning English. "Eat. No stand. Stand and eat no good. Understand?" Donn acknowledged that the Japanese had broached the matter to him before.

"What did you tell them?" I asked. "I told them I'd make a deal with them: we'd stop eating in the street if the Japanese would quit urinating there!"

Donn accepted the ribald as a valid part of life. His limericks and raunchy jokes livened up every party. Here is one he would have liked because it fools listeners into thinking they are ahead of the game when, in reality as in the martial arts, the words are only feints.

> There was a young lady named Tuck,
> Who had the most terrible luck;
> She went out in a punt,
> And fell over the front,
> And was bit in the leg by a duck.

Back during the early Fifties, after returning from Korea, Donn was second-in-command at the Inter-American Defense Fund housed in the pink Marshall Field mansion on 16th Street in Washington. He complained to me about the excessive social role he had to play helping his colonel host parties for the Washington elite. "How do you stand it?" I asked. "Easy," he said. He padded his role and cheated by funning. In the reception line glad-handing the upper crust, when the mighty introduced themselves Donn said he would smile hugely and double-talk amongst the din, "Oh, Mrs. Whitney (or some such), you miserable wretch, still whoring I see." And get away with it,

While Donn played the diplomat role with panache, he could be brusque on occasion. The chief editor for Tuttle years ago told me that he once was delicately talking to a famed writer, a Jesuit priest, about publishing his book. They were in a sumptuous office with the door open while halfway down the large outer room Donn was arguing at the desk of an editor about some textual overhaul the editor wanted to make on Donn's book. Donn never took kindly to editing and he was cussing like a Marine as he demonstrated some fighting technique that he didn't want expunged by the editor's blue pencil. The din rose to a crescendo and at its zenith, Donn came down on the corner of the desk with the technique in question, breaking the corner off while expostulating: "That is how the [obscenity] thing is done!"

Not too many yards away in the chief editor's office, the kindly little priest looked at my friend with some alarm and asked, "Shouldn't we have some police?" Red as a beet, my friend apologetically said, "Never mind. I'm afraid this is one of our own writers. You can understand, he is an artist and he feels more deeply than most people."

Another example of Donn's humor: one night at the Nationals in Los Angeles in 1955, during a hot-sake-in-a-saucer drinking contest with Kotani and other luminaries, he saved my life by showing me how to drink the stuff without letting too much go down. As in fighting, the trick was to fake with a lot of elbow and then shunt the liquor down your arm, sopping your sleeve and the floor. (But who noticed or cared?) Poor George Wilson, an old buddy from Seattle, never got in on the skinny. He held up magnificently all evening. Then he blinked once, widened his eyes, and fell over as though poleaxed. It took four of us to carry him off to bed that night and onto his plane the next morning.

Thanks to Donn I escaped that fate. However, remaining sober, feigning tipsy, presented another dilemma. The Japanese have the damnable custom of forcing everyone at a party to sing a song or declaim a poem solo. (I think I did James Whitcomb Riley's "Little Orphant Annie," on a previous occasion). Sloshing around on the floor feeling like Gene Kelly in *Singing in the Rain*, I told Donn I didn't dig that singing and was going to take a walk until it got over. Donn's brow furrowed, "You can't. If you don't show your ass, they'll lose face." I laughed at his attempt to impersonate anthropologist Ruth Benedict and turned to depart. He grabbed my arm. "Listen, I don't like it either. How about we do a duet?" So I sez how about "She'll Be Coming Round the Mountain When She Comes"? "OK by me." So we did, to tumultuous soused applause.

Donn loved to laugh. There was a time at the Meiji Club in Tokyo when we all told such stories that the waiters and other diners came over to our table, not to complain but to listen. At a corner table, the Deputy Chief of the US Embassy in Taipei was host to a dozen party-goers, out of earshot I thought. But a week later we lunched in Taipei and he mentioned that his group had enjoyed our party, even the dirty jokes told by the great big guy [Bluming]. I told him that this was the expatriate judo crew and that, actually, they had been relatively well behaved that night.

Partying at the Third Nationals in Los Angeles, 1955. Circling left to right: Donn Draeger, author, Ken Kuniyuki, Ben Ishii, Ken Yamada, unidentified man standing center back, unidentified man seated rear, Ray Moore, unidentified man, F. Miyazawa rear right, Shuzo Kato, unidentified man, and completing outer circle, George Wilson. Seated in center, San Furuta, Tadao Otaki, and Sumiyuki Kotani. *Photos courtesy of R. Smith.*

There was another aspect of the man—his hyperbole. While his research was rigorous and abided no exaggeration, he would sometimes stretch a tale to make a point. His safaris into Malaysia and elsewhere were done partly to collect data on archaeological weapon finds. He was trying to correlate these with human migrations. From the jungles he would often write of defeating local champions in free fighting. Some of this may indeed have happened, but the embellishments gave me pause. His tiger stories he never told me (he knew he couldn't con an old storyteller), but did tell friends of mine. There are two versions. In one, he was treed by a tiger, while in the other, he was treed by one tiger in the morning and a different tiger in the afternoon. How could he know they were different tigers? Even this, of course, may be attributed to his ready humor.

Donn and Sir Richard Burton, the legendary English explorer and scholar (1821-1890), shared an expertise in weaponry and neither was a stranger to hyperbole. Burton carried an iron walking stick as heavy as an elephant to keep fit. Donn treasured Burton's *The Book of the Sword*, and during his last years he asked me to send him a reprint. (The 1987 Dover reprint is still available.) Like its author, *The Book of the Sword* was idiosyncratic, strange, and sound. I'm sure Donn was also familiar with Burton's *The Sentiment of the Sword* (1911), an equally fascinating book. Burton here quotes Arab sources, "The lecture is one, the practice is a thousand," to show the primacy of green work over gray words. Here he tells that in teaching a new student, for the first month half an hour a day is ample provided there's not too much to unteach. After that, three half-hour sessions a week are sufficient. This light schedule seems to contradict his own experience for he writes in the same book that he began sword practice at twelve and sometimes had three practices a day. But the apparent contradiction may simply mean that over the years he found that, with a proper focus, long hours daily weren't required. Germanely, Burton said that he never let the pupil continue once he saw that he was fatigued, but also never let him sit down until he required rest. Burton was cognizant of iaido: "The sensible Japanese, who, holding the scabbard in the left hand, draws his sword with so little loss of time that he opens his man from belt to shoulder."

Burton decried form or ritual when carried beyond reality. ("Nothing is bad if it succeeds," said Burton in regard to proper form in fencing.) He noted that an overly-structured opponent often shouted loftily, "You touched my mask, my back, my arm!" without understanding that the mask touch could have gone through his brain, or six inches into his back. Therefore he replied just as loftily, "I touch what is before me and I'm amply satisfied with the result!"

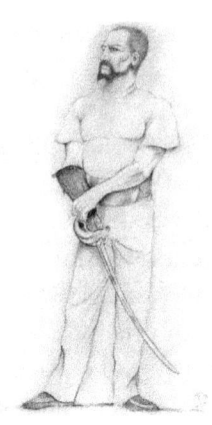

Sir Richard Burton.
Illustration by Oscar Ratti.

There was also a mystery to Donn Draeger. He almost never said anything about his personal affairs. Since I subscribed to Chesterton's philosophy that "the most sacred thing is to be able to close your own door," I never even thought of asking him. His past, his family—he never divulged anything of this, even when we'd sit around and talk about the halcyon past. And we did a lot of that. Almost everyone who'd gone through the Depression played the "Poor Game," for instance. In it, you let the other guy try to top your lowball. I'd say that when I was a kid we were so poor we used water instead of milk on our corn flakes. To which Donn would say, "What's corn flakes?" So I'd counter that when he was a babe his mom used baby powder on him, but that my mom was so poor she used Old Dutch Cleanser instead. Then he would top it all by telling how one Christmas Eve, his pa hadn't a quarter for presents, so went outside in the dark alley with a gun. (Like Billy Conn, the great light-heavyweight of the 1930s, Donn was twelve before he found out there were streets.) Those inside heard a single shot. A few minutes later, pa returned to tell the family that Santa Claus had just committed suicide.

Donn's fighting priorities changed over time. Early on, judo and kendo were the objects of his effort. After 1965, however, weaponry supplanted the judo. His mentor at the Tenshin Shoden Katori Shinto-ryu, Risuke Otake, said in an interview (Honolulu, Nov. 2, 1981) that when Donn entered his school fifteen years before, he was already 5th-dan judo, 7th-dan kendo, 7th-dan iaido, and a 7th-dan in jodo with *kyoshi*, or instructor's rank. Once he started doing Tenshin Shoden Katori Shinto-ryu, he stopped judo and kendo, his old sportive favorites.

Around 1966 Donn relocated to Narita, an hour outside Tokyo, where he remained for the rest of his life. The main reason for the change was to be nearer his new training. I have heard that Kodokan politics and specifically the new director of its foreign section, I. Abe, with whom Donn and some other foreign judoka had problems, may have contributed to his move. Donn still collected his mail and touched base at the Kodokan twice a week, but gone was the historic Ichigaya house and its nexus with the fascinating judoka who lived there.

Illustrative of Donn's giving is this incident told me by one of his students, Canadian Howard Alexander.

> In 1968, I went with Donn as a junior member to Indonesia for the summer to study Pentjak Silat. It was a wonderful learning experience for me. Donn and I started out earlier [from the rest of the group] and went by freighter through Hong Kong and Singapore and Jakarta. During the twelve days on that ship, Donn decided to teach me the uke for *kusarigama, jutte, tanjo jutsu,* and various *goshin* techniques. We also did many hours of jodo. We practiced about fifteen hours a day, only stopping for breakfast, lunch, and dinner, and for a couple of hours at midday when the steel decks were too hot to stand on. Even now remembering those twelve days, my arms ache and pain shoots through my wrists and elbows. One dark night with no moon, he took me on deck to practice jodo. I thought it was far too dark since I could hardly see anything but a shadow. But in true Donn fashion, he said, "It will train your sixth sense and reaction if you can't see your opponent." Needless to say, I couldn't hit him, but got smacked a number of times myself.

Draeger and mentor Otake Risuke engage in Katori Shinto-ryu Kenjutsu, at Katori Shrine in Chiba Prefecture, April 1978. *Photo courtesy of P. Lineberger.*

Donn had women friends but they didn't linger when they learned that his entire being was absorbed in the martial arts. I have it on good authority that he was married to a woman Marine once and that there was a son born before the union dissolved, but he never mentioned it. I'd always thought of Donn the military man as being conservative in his politics. (We were both too busy to talk politics though the few times we discussed Vietnam, he was as critical of US policy as I.) Yet here he is on military procurement (November 13, 1976):

> Damn, when I think of all the taxpayers' money going into things like the new super-duper tank development. I could cry. We need that monstrosity like a spare bridegroom at a wedding. When is the US going to get over its superlative complex—first, bigger, better? This damned tank [the future M1 Abrams] will only stimulate other nations to build a super-duper gun that will blast the super-duper hell out of our tank!

Like all friends, Donn and I had our differences. When Donn embarked on MAI, he began writing about overseas Chinese he'd met on his research trips throughout Southeast Asia. I did not think his articles and books on the martial arts and weapons of these regions approached his Japanese efforts. This had nothing to do with his branching into Chinese studies. In the past we had cut the pie so that he took Japan and I, China. That specialization was not sacrosanct. I didn't believe he was encroaching on my preserve. Instead, it was that I believed that the men and systems he showcased were inferior to those I studied under in Taiwan. I had visited the other areas and met their leading teachers and found them lacking. These teachers' tendency to slander superiors ("beat 'em any way you can!") added to my dislike for them. Singapore, Hong Kong, and Malaysia all boasted boxers who boosted themselves by disparaging Zheng Manqing (Cheng Man-ch'ing) and other Taiwan luminaries I had known.

Sadly, after listening to enough of them, Donn became confused. In a letter (July 6, 1974), he questioned my objectivity. He just couldn't believe that tiny Zheng Manqing could beat people the caliber of the huge Dutch judo champion Anton Geesink, the German wrestling champion W. Dietrich, and other people we knew. How could I believe it? He added that Wang Shuchin would not go onto a judo mat or a sumo ring or in an exchange with top swordsmen. He then said that the Chinese weren't great fighters historically. He had fought them in Korea and they weren't great warriors.

For Donn this was an impassioned statement. It was certainly not consistent with his earlier remarks on Masters Zheng and Wang. (Although, with more than a hint of hyperbole, he told many, but not me, that he had taken Wang's punch even when Wang wore his big ring!) Away from the Japanese orbit, Donn was out of his element. The locals pushed their wares and Donn bought too quickly.

One ingredient in this bias was his personal animus against the Chinese as a military power. He gained this prejudice serving on the ground during the Korean War, and his many Japanese martial art friends probably reinforced it. But this anti-Chinese prejudice was too sweeping. From 1830 to 1930, he was quite right about Chinese military frailty, "the weak man of Asia," and all that. But it wasn't a weak military power that pushed the United Nations forces from the Yalu River to the 38th Parallel. Further, one doesn't have to read Joseph Needham to know that during much of history the Chinese devoted more material and imaginative resources to war than anyone else. After all, the Chinese developed modern war from the fifth to the third centuries BCE, and then waged it on a scale that Europe did not achieve until the nineteenth century CE.

Donn's protestation contrasts also with what he said during his lecture "The Role of Sword in Japanese Martial Arts" given in Honolulu on March 30, 1976:

> There is much development on ki studies currently. Not to slur anyone, but the Japanese know little about ki. The Chinese know, and the Japanese would do well to sit at their feet. This would take a lot of humility. No Japanese, including Mr. Tohei, claims to know how to use ki to absorb punishment. This is a significant Japanese failure, and they are still in primary school in this regard. The Japanese have their ethnic pride, of course, and they must suppress it or they'll never learn very much. If they were to develop some aspect of ki beyond the Chinese it would merely be by coincidence. Therefore, if you want to learn about ki find a qualified Chinese.

Master Otake with short stick (*jo*) and his senior, Donn Draeger, have at it.

Photo courtesy of the International Hoplology Society, P. Lineberger.

Puzzled, I wrote Donn to say that I too had believed as he did, even after being completely defeated in pushing-hands as well as in free and unstructured skirmishes. But the fact remained: Zheng had never been beaten in challenges. When I asked Zheng how he would have handled sumotori, judoka, and wrestlers, he acknowledged the physics problem. He said that he would tell a challenger that he could hit or kick, but if he grabbed his small body, Zheng would have to resort to *dianxue* (the art of striking vital points). I then suggested to Donn that he hop a plane down and I would set something up. Zheng had some tests such as turning his arm over while preventing the other from doing the same to him at which no one had beaten him, and I thought this would persuade Donn. If it didn't, Zheng would be amenable to a free fight.

As if his statements had been a momentary lapse, Donn wrote four months later that there was no need for him to test Mr. Zheng, though Jon Bluming might consider it. Then, ambiguously, he said, "Short of a fight to do somebody or myself, in, I am not equipped to test anybody." Donn seems here to mix testing and fighting. Actually, he would have enjoyed the tests. Professor Zheng could take your hand, as in shaking hands, and turn it over or prevent you from turning his over, beating you without regard for your body weight or weightlifting ability. Or if you liked striking he would trade chops on the other's arm. He had never lost in either test. Or in a fight.

Shimizu Takaji in the early 1970s, headmaster of Shindo Muso-ryu and Donn's personal teacher. *Photo from the T. Shimizu Archives.*

Donn Draeger and Kobayashi Sensei of Shindo Muso-ryu Jojutsu. Photo taken May 1978 at the Botokuden, Kyoto. *Photos courtesy of the International Hoplology Society, P. Lineberger.*

I once asked a judo-cum-karate teacher who studied in New York City how he had done at pushing-hands with Professor Zheng. Alone of all Zheng's students, big or small, fast or slow, he told me that he never really tried to push Zheng in push-hands. "He was an old man," but he was sure he could have pushed Zheng if he had tried. I bluntly told him that I and bigger and better guys than the two of us had thought the same thing and had been vigorously "managed" and handed our heads by Zheng. I added that in not trying, he had missed the biggest thrill of his taiji life. But he went away unconvinced. I even suggested a ready test. He should brace Ben Lo, who had just come to America. If he could handle Ben in pushing-hands, then perhaps he could beat Zheng. But if Ben beat him or it were a tie, he should forget it. Ben has great skill but never attained Zheng's level.

He never took me up on that test. Thinking about it now, I realize why neither he nor Donn—both fine fellows—would not pursue the test. Either consciously or deep down, their egos would not permit them to ever know that their years in the more or less "hard" arts availed nothing against a soft, old man. Ego, that monkey on all our backs, prevented them from ever knowing that Laozi (Lao Tzu) was right in saying that the soft overcomes the hard. Sure, one finds it in the Gospels at a once remove, but where other than in Zheng Manqing did these friends of mine ever have a chance to see it physically demonstrated?

It remains a pity.

The mystery attending Donn continued to the end. We stayed in touch swimmingly until his June 1981 letter saying that he'd just returned from two months in "Lulu" (Honolulu) where he'd worked on the Hoplology Center's legal status and International Judo Federation matters.

> That was part of my time in Lulu. The other, which I'd rather not go into detail about, was the fiasco with the VA [Veterans Administration], Tripier [Army Medical Center], and my badly broken foot. Everybody decided it needed an operation but after the total time, I got no farther than a hospital bed: one hour before operation it was canceled and I was told to go now—Geeezzzzz!

That sounded ominous.

Eight months later in February 1982, Peter Nichols, one of my taiji students, who was studying under Donn at the University of Hawaii, phoned me about Donn's physical decline. Peter was driving Donn to class and was mortified one day when, on an errand, he had parked some distance from the store to which they were going. They began walking and Donn, erect as ever, was struggling to keep up. Peter tried to get him to pause while he went back for the car.

Donn would have none of it, and they made it to the store. Donn could barely walk and couldn't train. He told Peter that tests proved nothing and drugs, which Donn abhorred, had not helped. The brass at Tripier Army Medical Center now wanted to try a toxic drug [adriamycin] that might harm his heart. They gave him a week to decide. I already had been alerted to the problem by Donn's senior students and was working with a judoka, Dr. Tom Malone, acting head of the National Institutes of Health in Bethesda, on his behalf.

Previous page: Shindo Muso-ryu members in Hawaii, 1981. Left to right: D. Draeger Sensei, Quintin Chambers Sensei, Pat Lineberger, Bob Valdez, and Peter Nichols. *Photo courtesy of the International Hoplology Society.*

His May 11, 1982 letter was the last one I got from Donn:

> Many, many thanks for your work on finding out something positive at Bethesda. Tomorrow I am on my way back to Tripier and after consultations I will know more and be back in touch with you again. At the moment I am in bad shape; hardly able to walk or stay up for long periods of time. Tripier's plans may well be to IV me with the antibiotic called adriamycin which in itself was ruled out earlier because they did not like my heart condition said to be either tricuspid insufficiency or mitral valve trouble. The biotic [sic] is famous for ruining hearts and without any guarantee of aiding my liver condition, I have held off until now. Wish I had other opinions for Tripier is all one opinion. The edema in my legs is now into my abdominal region to the point of bursting (no fooling) and I hasten to get back before some complication sets in. You'll hear from me after I consult Tripier.

I immediately phoned him. It was a sad thing. In a frustrated but healthy voice, he told me of the wards of the dying at Tripler and how humiliating it was to die an inch at a time. Dr. Malone had at last got the top man in the field to treat Donn, and an obscenity of a man he was, with all the warmth of an iceberg. But by the time I relayed word back to him through his seniors, Donn had chosen to return to a Veterans Hospital near his step-brother's home in Wisconsin, and died shortly thereafter.

Donn was a warrior on pain. He had to be. Pat Lineberger, one of his deshi, tells me that Donn had severe allergic reactions to any type of painkiller. Which meant if he had surgery he could have no anesthetics. In 1978 while he was in Honolulu for a lecture series he had to have a root canal done. And did it sans pain-killer. Another time he was on the operating table for surgery on a big toe that had plagued him for years. He insisted on no anesthetic and told them to proceed. The doctors were stupefied but when Donn stuck to his guns they canceled surgery! That toe was later caught in a door at Tripier Army Hospital that another fellow accidentally slammed. Donn felt intense pain at first, but then it disappeared. He laughed in recalling that the door had corrected what the aborted surgery was supposed to do.

Back to the mystery. Death, of course, is the biggest one. We all know that we must die but deny it will happen to ourselves, despite Saint Theresa's "We are all going to die in a couple hours." In August 1985, a Chinese-

American Army doctor in Hawaii, a student of Donn's, phoned me. His examination of Donn had revealed swollen legs and a carcinoma that, as I recall, had metastasized from his intestines to his liver. The doctor said that Donn thought he had been poisoned during his trip to Malaysia. If true—Donn may have guessed wrong—we will never know whether it was intentionally done or a misadventure of diet.

There can be no mystery, however, in how he benefited America and the world by his contributions. He opened Asian combatives to the full view of the West. He was an authentic warrior able to blend the tough with the tender. He could fight the match, referee it, and then explain the mechanics of it later in his books. He was an unusual American-he never made a dollar with his incomparable skill. All of it went into the more than thirty books we have inherited. Hear his name. Donn Draeger: Don't nod in recognition; Donn Draeger: "Bow with admiration and respect."

Richard Hayes, the hoplologist, said it for all of us in his poem:

> Draeger no kami
> domiciled in that old snag
> high on the hill
> domo arigato gozaimasu.*

* "Thank you very much."

Acknowledgment

A special thanks goes to Donn Draeger's top deshi Hunter Armstrong, Jodo Federation of Malaysia, Pat Lineberger, and others who have provided illustrations, technical assistance and advice for this chapter.

Note: This chapter is an extract from Robert W. Smith's book, *Martial Musings: A Portrayal of Martial Arts in the 20th Century*, published by Via Media Publishing.

— 2 —

Letters on Miyamoto Musashi
by Donn F. Draeger

Illustrations by Oscar Ratti.
© 1999 *Futuro Designs & Publications*

Introduction

The following is the result of merging and editing two letters (September 2, 1969 and June 29, 1981) that Donn F. Draeger wrote to Robert W. Smith. Joseph Svinth did the editing by permission of Robert W. Smith.

The letters' background is this. In the spring of 1981, Smith decided to review Kodansha's recently released translation of Yoshikawa Eiji's novel *Musashi*. First, however, he asked his collaborator on *Asian Fighting Arts* for his opinion of the historical Musashi. The result was the following essay, most of which appeared in a typewritten aerogram dated June 29, 1981. The 1969 letter mentioned only referred to Musashi's underrated skill at jujutsu.

Editorially, paragraphing was added and a few sentences were moved about. (Which is hardly surprising, inasmuch as one tends to get lax about paragraphing when typing on aerograms!). Otherwise the article's vibrant style reflects the typically ebullient tone of Draeger's correspondence with Smith.

— Draeger's Letters —

Regarding Miyamoto Musashi, most historians will allow that he was a historical person, but his dates are in contention. I follow Watatani with 1584(?) to 1645. The date of death seems well established. During his lifetime, at least four other persons are known to have used his name. Why not, with so famous a man?

The historical Musashi was foremost an enigmatic character. Most of what is written about him, or credited to him, is fiction. For example, he did not write the *Gorin no sho*. Those who came after and eulogized him did the writing. This was much like the Bible, Qur'an, etc., where students recalled the great man's sayings and statements plus whatever embellishments the writers wished to add. The result was the *Gorin no sho* we have today.

In its recent Japanese editions, the *Gorin no sho* has been misinterpreted and recast in terms that are glowing and pleasing to modern ears. Thus, it is a far cry from any original that may have once existed. Even the earliest version, the one that never gets to the public's eyes, is far removed from the brush or mouth of its purported author. Instead, it has a Tokugawa-era (1600-1868) Neo-Confucian tone.

Musashi himself was not the strongest *kengo* (sword expert) of his time. He allegedly acknowledged the superiority of a Shinkage-ryu master of his

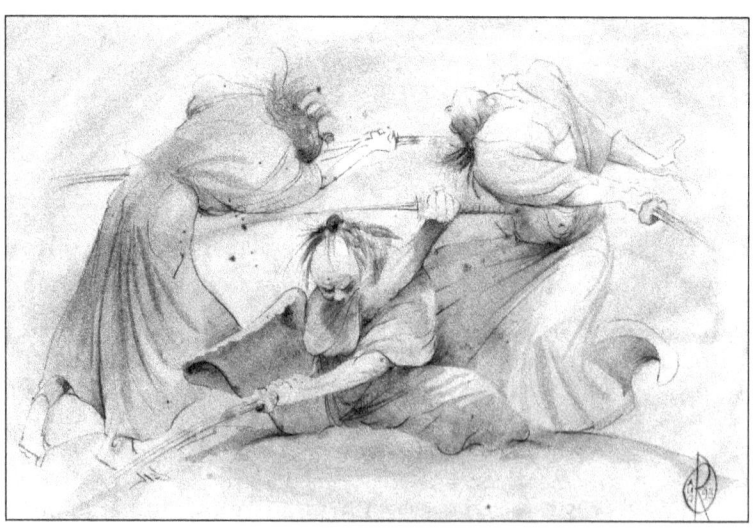

own time. There were many stronger before and after him.

He did not devise the *nita* or two-sword manner of combat. This had already been devised and was in use about two centuries before he was born. Tenshin Shoden Katori Shinto-ryu was using the two-sword method (*ryo-ta*) in combat during the earlier Muromachi period (1338-1573).

Qualified authorities today regard the artifacts allegedly made by Musashi such as the *tsuba*, or sword guard, as not made by him, but possibly designed by him. That famous self-portrait is suspect. The reason is that the face shows, among other things, tension, rage, and defiance. These are all qualities that good swordsmanship proscribes, and are contradictory to what is considered a good budo face. Certainly they are directly contradictory to the concepts expressed in the *Gorin no sho*. Only the equally famed painting of the shrike on a branch may be legitimately from his hands.

As for his technical skills, today's authorities in the classical martial traditions (*koryu*) make nothing special of him. To them he is just another swordsman, not particularly the best, but admittedly the best advertised. That the man was famous, but the details of his life largely unknown, make him a fitting place upon which to hang whatever an author wants to say.

Something that puts the historical Musashi high above the run-of-the-mill armchair theorist, however, is that he was a fighting man who had seen combat on the losing side at Sekigahara. I also have found evidence that he was an extremely competent jujutsuka. The latter never gets play due to the popular emphasis on his swordsmanship.

What one finds written about Musashi today is almost wholly fiction. Kodansha's English translation of *Gorin no sho*, called *A Book of Five Rings*, is technically bad. The reason it was accepted was that the publishers knew nothing about swordsmanship. Yoshikawa's novels serialized in the Japanese newspapers during the late 1930s and recently reprinted by Kodansha are a sourcebook of errors, some deliberate, some innocent. Together they have probably permanently damaged chances for the public to ever understand the truth about the man and add up to near disaster for the scholar or researcher who is not extremely careful about his sources.

In sum, Musashi was a loner, an eccentric, a capable swordsman, and a man of artistic sensibilities about whose life the truth is not well known. Nevertheless, he lives on in the words of romantic novelists and other imaginative writers. The latter idealized Musashi satisfies perhaps all but the most critical readers as to what the ideal image of the classical Japanese warrior must be.

An Editor's Guide to Further Reading

There are at least four English-language translations of *The Book of Five Rings* currently available. Listed alphabetically by translators, they are:

Cleary, T. (1993). Boston: Shambhala.
Harris, V. (1974). Woodstock, NY: Overlook Press.
Kaufman, S. (1994). Rutland, VT: Charles E. Tuttle.
Nihon Services Corporation (1983). New York: Bantam Books.

The translation by Kaufman makes Musashi sound as if he was a late twentieth century karate teacher rather than a seventeenth century Japanese swordsman. Meanwhile, the translation by Nihon Services Corporation makes Musashi sound as if he was a graduate of Harvard Business School rather than a seventeenth century Japanese swordsman. As a result, students of the Japanese sword arts probably will prefer the translations by Cleary and Harris.

Books that can help readers correct for the errors inherent in any translation of Musashi's *Gorin no sho* include:

Cleary, T. (1991). *The Japanese Art of War: Understanding the culture of strategy*. Boston and London: Shambhala.
Draeger, D. (1973). *Classical bujutsu* (*Martial Arts and Ways of Japan*), *volume 1*. New York: Weatherhill.
Kammer, R. (1986). *The way of the sword: The Tengu-geijutsu-ron of Chozan Shissai*. Translated from the German by Betty J. Fitzgerald. London: Arkana.
Yagyu Muneyori (1986). *The sword and the mind*. Translated from the Japanese by Hiroaki Sato. Woodstock, NY: Overlook Press.

— 3 —

Donn Draeger & the International Hoplology Society

by H. E. Davey

Above: the late Donn Draeger (right) demonstrating a kata of the Shindo Muso-ryu in Hawaii. *Photo courtesy of W. Muromoto & Tengu Press.* Right: Finding time for sword practice while on ship, Draeger stops briefly for a photograph. *Photo courtesy of Hunter Armstrong.*

In 1973 and 1974, a three-volume set of books, dealing with Japanese martial arts was presented to the English-speaking public. The books were titled, *Classical Bujutsu, Classical Budo,* and *Modern Bujutsu and Budo.* Concentrating on accurate, detailed information about the legitimate history, philosophy, and training methods of classical as well as traditional Japanese martial arts, they proved to be immensely popular. Providing first-hand accounts of the actual nature of authentic *budo* (martial ways) and *bujutsu* (martial arts), the volumes remain virtually unsurpassed and serve to rekindle interest in an old academic discipline—hoplology—the study of the origins, patterns, relationships and phenomenology of combative behavior at all levels of social complexity. Many of the Americans and Europeans who have read these books will never think about the martial arts in the same way again.

It is not an exaggeration to state that Donn F. Draeger, author of these books and numerous others, can be credited with establishing the martial arts, in the eyes of Westerners, as genuine cultural arts and in a manner that no one else has before or since. It seems that nearly every serious book about the martial arts, particularly publications relating to traditional budo/bujutsu, contains at least one quote attributed to Mr. Draeger. Surprisingly, almost nothing has been written about him. This is in spite of the fact that he acted as John Wayne's double in "The Barbarian and the Geisha," doubled for Sean Connery in the 1967 James Bond film, "You Only Live Twice," and was a stunt choreographer for both films. Yet, the average martial artist knows little about this enigmatic man or his exclusive, world-wide group of associates.

Meik Skoss uses a staff to counter a naginata. Skoss studied and conducted research with Donn Draeger in Japan and Souteast Asia. *Photos courtesy of Franz Gaschler.*

Donn F. Draeger as Hoplologist

Donn Draeger was born in 1922. In Chicago, at the early age of seven, he began to study traditional jujutsu under a Japanese instructor. He would later take up the practice of Kodokan judo, and throughout his life, he served as an ardent proponent of classical judo, that is, judo as a method of mental and physical cultivation, as envisioned by the art's founder, Kano Jigoro. Draeger's contributions to judo were many. According to the *Official AAU-USJF Judo Handbook*, published in 1970,

> Donn F. Draeger is one of the pioneers responsible for the original efforts to develop and systematize national and international judo. As a co-founder of the first national judo body, the Amateur Judo Association, Mr. Draeger later played an active role in the establishment of the Judo Black Belt Federation (USJF), co-founded the Pan-American Judo Federation (currently the Pan-American Judo Union), founded and developed the East Coast Black Belt Association, as well as several clubs in the eastern U.S.A. Mr. Draeger now makes the Orient his home, where, during the past decade and more, he has become one of the world's foremost authorities on Asian weapons and fighting arts. He is currently conducting doctoral research in his major field of speciality, the origins and philosophy of Japanese martial arts and ways.
>
> – Pohl, 1970: 243

Draeger would become one of the highest-ranking Western judo practitioners in the world, serve as a liaison between the famed Kodokan Judo Institute of Tokyo and the U.S. Judo Federation, and teach as a member of the elite Kodokan staff. Among American judo instructors, perhaps only Walter Todd, an old acquaintance of Draeger's and an eighth-degree black belt, has had an equally distinguished judo career. Todd, like Draeger, lived in Japan for several years and, like Draeger, studied directly under Mifune Kyuzo, Ito Kazuo, and Sato Shizuya, all legendary judo experts.

Draeger's primary career was in the military, and before his retirement, he rose to the rank of Major in the U.S. Marine Corps. Starting in the early 1940s, Draeger lived and traveled in the Pacific Basin as well as in the continental and insular areas of Asia. In the mid-1950s, he took up permanent residence in Japan, where he became absorbed in the study of budo/bujutsu. Draeger eventually studied and earned advanced teaching credentials in a large number of combative arts and weapons systems including, but not limited to, judo, sword, sword-drawing, staff, glaive, spear, and empty-handed systems of Tenshin Shoden Katori Shinto-ryu, stick and sword systems of Shindo Muso-ryu, and *jukendo* (the art of the bayonet). C.W. Nicol, author of *Moving Zen–Karate as a Way to Gentleness*, who met Donn Draeger in Japan in the early 1960s, describes him in the following passage:

> And so the time was right to meet a man who would largely change my way of life. In fact I had already met him on the dojo mats. He was the big American who criticized my judo breakfalls. Donn Draeger, sixth degree black belt in judo, sixth degree black belt in *jojutsu* [stick fighting] and black belt rank in a dozen other martial arts. Tall, extremely muscular, upright, with piercing eyes and a quick, easy laugh, Donn is a most impressive man. He is also a very gentle man, quick to help a student, tell a joke when needed, help out a friend or a stranger.
> – Nicol, 1975: 25-26

Supporting himself by teaching English and through his military pension, Draeger felt very much at home in Japan and, more than most foreigners, he was eventually treated as a peer by many senior-ranking members of the Japanese martial arts community. It was a unique situation, involving a unique individual, who as Nicol has stated, "had fought in the Pacific war, seen friends die beside him on the beaches of Iwo Jima, faced and killed Japanese under circumstances of hate, and yet here was a man who loved and respected the Japanese, who understood that gentleness was the way of the warrior. Bigotry is left to those people on the fringe" (Nicol, 1970: 25-26).

Gradually, Draeger's attention was drawn to one of Japan's oldest cultural organizations for the study of classical budo/bujutsu, the *Nihon Kobudo Shinkokai* (Society for the Promotion of Ancient Japanese Martial Arts and Ways), an exclusive association in which he gained membership. Draeger next founded the International Research Section of the Nihon Kobudo Shinkokai, in which non-Japanese would be able to study and conduct research within the Japanese martial ethos. At this time, Draeger also began assembling the fundamental conceptual framework of modern hoplology, the systematic study of mankind's combative culture in all ages. By the early 1960s, this section of the Nihon Kobudo Shinkokai had already conducted an ongoing series of investigations in Japan and had produced a sizable amount of hoplological data which was mainly, but not exclusively, relevant to Japan. Draeger soon changed the title and modified the activities of the original International Research Section to create a more broadly based organization, which, after several name changes, became the International Hoplological Research Center (IHRC). Pioneer fieldworkers further widened the scope of the organization's activities, and several hoplological expeditions were made into Australia and the Indonesian Archipelago (Draeger, n.d.: 3).

The Rebirth of Hoplology

In many ways, Sir Richard F. Burton (1821-1890) may be considered the doyen of hoplologists, due to his efforts in the nineteenth century to organize hoplology as a body of knowledge with its own unique terms, concepts, and methodology. No single discipline, he believed, was capable of embracing the emergence and evolution of social humans and their cultural contrivances. Thus, Sir Burton devoted his life to the development of another "window"—hoplology—through which to view the complexities of mankind. It is, however, through the efforts of Draeger that hoplology, a venerable but somewhat dormant discipline, re-emerged in the late 1960s to gain academic support as a well-established field with specific aims and research strategies.

However, it is important to emphasize that, despite the IHRC's study of mankind's combative nature and culture, it was not a sort of "think-tank for warmongers." Hoplology does not encourage war-like behavior, but rather studies the nature and effects of such behavior:

> Whether we believe that war is beneficial to society or that it may cause society to disintegrate, war continues to make history. It continues to be the arbiter when all else fails. Man today, as in the past, finds it necessary to label his wars, on the basis of expedient morality, as either "just" or "unjust." Both these words, however, defy attempts at universal definitions. Most decisions to wage war are based on might, not right, and rarely is war a moral issue, though rationalization seeks to make it so. For the reckless man, the horrors of war are its fascination, while for the careful man wars are counsels of despair.
> – Draeger, 1973a: 12

One of Draeger's main goals, and an objective of present-day hoplologists, is to understand how combative skills have influenced civilization or, as Draeger wrote in *Classical Bujutsu*, "It is doubtful whether the Japanese people and the country as a whole can really be understood or appreciated by anyone without a degree of knowledge of their martial culture" (Draeger, 1973b: 14). This statement would, naturally, hold true for other nations as well.

Draeger's elite organization carried its operations into the Pacific Basin area and the Greater Malay Archipelago in the 1970s, and members of the IHRC traveled outside of Japan to introduce and explain the "new" discipline of hoplology. Draeger himself spent considerable time at the esteemed East-West Center of Hawaii and the University of Hawaii in Honolulu, lecturing at both institutions, developing professional contacts between the IHRC and scholars in various fields, and performing research through the help of federal grants. Draeger and several associates also produced a report entitled *Classical*

Hawaiian Martial Culture for the East-West Center and the Bernice P. Bishop Museum in Honolulu. For the rest of his life, Draeger would concentrate on that segment of human culture concerned with weapons, armor, combative accoutrements, and fighting systems, not only with regard to their technical characteristics, but also the ways in which they interact with the economic, political, social, and religious institutions of human societies.

The emergence of the IHRC was a boon to researchers, not only in hoplology, but also in numerous fields of research intersecting this discipline. The group concentrated on producing data in the following areas:

- **TECHNICAL HOPLOLOGY: The study of environmental factors, materials, and production processes and their relationship to the development of weapons, armor, and combative accoutrements.**

While this area of hoplology concentrates on the identification of natural agents that condition the making of weapons, it also includes a study of the impact of weapons on the environment. Great consideration is also given to the conservation of extant weapons and their methods of display and storage.

- **FUNCTIONAL HOPLOLOGY: The study of the structure and organization of combative systems.**

This area of research includes the analysis and classification of combative systems, taking into consideration the functional application in each system's design and evolution. Training patterns are closely observed in terms of their relationships to real and idealized applications. This area also includes investigations of the reciprocal relationships between weapons and combative systems.

- **BEHAVIORAL HOPLOLOGY: The study of the psychological and physiological factors in humanity's combativeness and the development of combative capabilities.**

This includes the investigation of the variables which influence the evolution of combative systems, e.g., studies of the historical process and genealogical factors connected with the inventors and founders of weapons and combative systems. A unique development in this area of hoplology theoretics is the identification of the "adaptive traits," which infuse all combative behaviors in modern people as well as their hominid ancestors. These traits are viewed in phylogenetic perspective, and in relation to the phenomenology of combat and the use of weapons.

This area also covers the socio-cultural roles and effects of weapons and combative systems on the individual and the collective social organization. It includes the identification and description of mankind's martial belief systems and their corresponding social and institutional import. The analysis of behavior related to weapons and combative systems as well as the study of linguistics in the evolution of combative culture is also included in this area of study.

Founding of the International Hoplology Society

Draeger, who lived at various times in Japan, China, Mongolia, Korea, Malaysia, and Indonesia, remained the founder and Director of the International Hoplological Research Center in Tokyo until his death in 1982. In 1983, Hunter B. Armstrong, a close associate of Draeger's, as well as a practitioner of the Japanese martial arts, succeeded Draeger as the Director of the IHRC, which was renamed the International Hoplology Society (IHS) in 1986. In 1992, the IHS was incorporated as a non-profit organization in Hawaii. The IHS currently owns a library consisting of over 1,000 volumes dealing with hoplology and related disciplines; over 50,000 photographs and negatives that are the results of numerous field trips to various Pacific Basin and Asian continental countries; and a large collection of weapons and related artifacts, totaling more than 500 items. Several databases are also being developed. Of course, the accurate preservation, study, and understanding of various countries' martial arts and combative cultures is a major objective of the IHS. This is vital, as relatively few people seem to fully grasp the true nature and value of many civilizations' martial arts:

> The exponent of today's modern budo gropes about in a maze of classical traditions that he does not understand, and thus, the cleverest of his kind declare that the classical disciplines must be freed from feudal Japanese superstitions and raised to great heights of rational efficiency so as to yield wealth, prestige, and practical use. Some foreigners proudly declare that they aim to "Americanize," or otherwise nationalize, Japanese budo in terms more suited to their country's way of life. Most foreigners have selfish aims that they disguise by mouthing lofty phrases that are nothing but lip service. The Western trainee also expects to reach a high degree of technical skill and leadership without first having shown his personal soundness through his cultivation of ideals. He trains with varying degrees of sincerity, albeit rigorously. But he does not really know through experience the hardship that is a companion to frugal living and so necessary in the lives of exponents of the classical disciplines. He is quite unable to relinquish the comfortable, easy ways of doing his (for example) "American" style of budo. His dojo is the very personification of his egocentric and flamboyant aims. It is always filled with display; in it will be found finery, murals, the excessive use of

pictures, nonutilitarian objects, and decorations, all of which operate as distractions and guarantee the exponents training there every opportunity to miss the intrinsic purpose of training.

– Draeger, 1974: 181

Clearly, this passage was designed to provoke a reaction from, in this instance, practitioners of modern budo, but similar difficulties will most likely be in store for any cultural art that is in the process of "transplanting itself onto foreign soil." In fact, Draeger's occasional sharp denunciations of Western followers of the Asian martial arts stemmed from his years of training in them and his profound realization that, in the case of budo,

Metaphysically speaking, the *do* forms urge their advocates to seek an understanding of the whole of life through a segment of it, a sphere of personal activity in which the cadence of nature can be sensed and experienced. The *do* forms thus involve transferring an attitude toward life from the particular to the universal and absolute. . . . they act only as the vehicles by which the individual can reach his goal, only "helps" toward that last decisive "leap to enlightenment" that culminates in self-perfection.

– Draeger, 1993: 25

Draeger, therefore, desired that the IHRC serve not only as an institution whereby individuals could research the effects of combative behavior on culture, but also as a means by which martial artists could discover their historical/cultural roots and the true value of their chosen discipline. As the legitimate successor to the IHRC, the IHS strives to accomplish the same purposes.

The IHS is an entirely independent, non-profit organization and offers its services to scholars, universities, museums, collectors, private and governmental organizations, writers, and publishers around the world. It is not devoted to any particular combative discipline and does not offer ranking in any martial art. Instead, its activities include field research trips to various parts of the world for the collection of hoplological data (written materials, direct video and audio recordings of extant systems, artifacts, etc.), the establishment of a library storage facility where such data can be made available to researchers, and the ongoing development of the study of hoplology. All activities of the group are under the aegis of the IHS Director and the IHS Advisory Committee (currently headed by David A. Hall, Ph.D.), the members of which have earned international prestige in hoplology, arms and armor studies, modern military and police studies, and various academic disciplines related to hoplology.

The IHS has recently relocated its headquarters to Arizona after being based for several years in Hawaii. It continues to publish the society's journal *HOPLOS*, a number of monographs that are transcriptions of lectures presented by Draeger at the University of Hawaii as well as at seminars in Malaysia, and *The IHS Guide to Classical Martial Ryu of Japan*. Through the efforts of the International Hoplology Society, Inc., the continued development, growth, and preservation of Donn Draeger's legacy is ensured.

Hunter B. Armstrong, IHS Director, demonstrating the classical use of the spear in Owari Kan-ryu. *Photos courtesy of H. Armstrong.*

A Special Thanks
from the author and publisher to Hunter Armstrong for his kind assistance in providing materials and information for this article and to Franz Gaschler and Wayne Muromoto for the rare photographs.

References
Draeger, D., Armstrong, H., and Hall, D. (n.d.). *The international hoplology society*. Kamuela, HI: International Hoplology Society, Inc.

Draeger, D. (1973). *Classical budo*. New York: John Weatherhill, Inc.

Draeger, D. (1973). *Classical bujutsu*. New York: John Weatherhill, Inc.

Draeger, D. (1974). *Modern budo and bujutsu*. New York: John Weatherhill, Inc.

Nicol, C. (1975). *Moving Zen–Karate as a way to gentleness*. New York: Dell Publishing.

Pohl, D. (Ed.). (1970). *Official AAU-USJF judo handbook*. Detroit, MI: United States Judo Federation.

— 4 —

Donald F. Draeger's Wisconsin Grave
by H. Richard Frimanm Ph.D.

*Photograph courtesy
of H. Richard Friman.*

Donald (Donn) F. Draeger shaped the lives of several generations of martial artists. A few lucky ones knew him personally as mentor, teacher, and friend. Others met him briefly in training halls or saw him participate in demonstrations around the world. His books and articles define serious scholarship in the martial arts to this day.

I found Donn Draeger's writings one Tokyo afternoon in 1984 at the library of the International House of Japan. I had been exploring different areas of the martial arts for nine years, but until that moment I had never really understood why, or what I was seeking. From Donn Draeger's published work I learned that the core of the martial arts and ways is a search for knowledge. The search leads to traditions and teachers, questions and answers and, if we are lucky, to a sense of how much there is to learn.

One thing about this search is the discovery that the world can be a small place and our paths can take interesting turns. On June 2, 1998, I discovered that Donn Draeger was buried in the Wood National Cemetery, in Milwaukee, Wisconsin, ten minutes from my dojo, twenty minutes from my house, fourteen hours from Japan and fourteen years from that library in Tokyo.

The cemetery traces its existence to the 1860s, and includes among its noteworthy sites the graves of Buffalo Soldiers and of Medal of Honor winners from the American Civil War. Donn Draeger's grave site is located in an older section of the cemetery on the fringes of the veterans complex and is marked, like many, by a nondescript stone. The facilities of Wood National Cemetery were closed to new, "full-casket burials" in 1996 and since that time veterans have been laid to rest in newer cemeteries in more prominent locations.

The cemetery is bisected by Interstate 94, Wisconsin's major highway. It is barely visible from the road, offering motorists a fleeting image overshadowed by an aging baseball stadium, parking lots, and the skeleton of a new stadium under construction. Seven older sections of the cemetery are accessible only by a narrow road with hairpin turns, small bridges, and partially rusted gates. Donn Draeger's grave lies here, in a section of the cemetery recently under consideration for possible relocation. The relocation proposals have faded for the moment but remain a possibility in the continuous deliberations concerning the endless expansion of Wisconsin's interstate system.

Donn Draeger's death in October 1982 at the Wood National Hospital in Milwaukee attracted little attention. Martial artists active in Wisconsin during the early 1980s were unaware that he was even in the United States.

Left: Kaminoda Tsunemori Sensei paying his respects at Drager's grave side. Right: Guests making a spiritual offerings (left to right): T. Koyama, T. Kaminoda, C. Warren, H. Friman, C. Gilmore, and T. Kato. *Photos courtesy of T. Kaminoda.*

The connection between Donn Draeger and Wisconsin was not very clear. On several occasions during the early 1990s, I had traveled to Rick Polland's Rembukan dojo in Baltimore to participate in jodo training. Originally from Wisconsin, Polland had expressed his belief that Donn Draeger's family was located in the town of West Bend, and so possibly his grave was there as well. West Bend is roughly one hour north of Milwaukee. My initial inquiries, however, met with little success.

When I was in Tokyo some years later, in May 1998, the real search began at the request of Kaminoda Tsunemori Sensei (Menkyo Kaiden, Shindo Musoryu Jodo; Jodo 8th-dan Hanshi, Zen Nihon Kendo Renmei [ZNKR]; Iaido 8th-dan Hanshi, ZNKR; Kendo 7th-dan Kyoshi, ZNKR). During a discussion after jodo practice, Kaminoda Sensei said that since I was from Wisconsin I should try to find Donn Draeger's grave. I promised to do so. Kaminoda Sensei and Draeger Sensei had trained together in jodo and other budo for 26 years. In 1970, along with the influential Shimizu Takaji Sensei (Menkyo Kaiden, Shindo Muso-ryu Jodo; Menkyo Kaiden, Shinto-ryu Kenjutsu, Ikkaku-ryu Jutte-jutsu, Isshin Ryu Kusarigama-jutsu, Ittatsu-ryu Hojo-jutsu, Uchida-ryu Tanjo-jutsu; Hanshi, Jodo), they had visited the United States spreading their knowledge of classical martial arts and ways. Twelve years later, Donn Draeger, in poor health, would return to the United States. He never returned to Japan.

A week later, back in Milwaukee an initial search through reels of microfilmed cemetery records proved futile. With visions of walking through every cemetery in Washington County in a search for grave markers, I drove to the town of West Bend where, on a whim, I decided to stop first at the West Bend Public Library. If Donn Draeger did have family in the area, perhaps the local newspaper would have printed an obituary notice. Four reels of microfilm later, I found a brief notice in the West Bend News of October 26, 1982. Donald F. Draeger had died in the Veteran's Hospital in Wood, Wisconsin and was interred in Wood National Cemetery, Milwaukee.

Driving back to Milwaukee was a blur. I was speeding, as if somehow Donn Draeger's grave would no longer be there if I didn't hurry. The roads of the veterans complex are scenic, serene, and confusing. Despite information from the cemetery office, I twice missed the turnoff for the section containing Draeger's grave. The narrow winding road led to a small parking space which I had seen every day on the way home from work, never wondering what it was.

I walked down the rows of grave sites reading the markers. The dates were in no particular order. Wars and deaths do not always coincide, a veteran's irony that creates a patchwork of names and histories. Donald F. Draeger, veteran of World War II and Korea, born April 15, 1922, died

October 20, 1982, lies among these warriors on a sloping green hillside. Standing beside the grave, I was torn between elation and sadness. The joy of discovery gave way to the sorrow of reflection. As I looked around, I couldn't help thinking that Draeger deserved much more than this.

Gone but not forgotten, Draeger receives visitors. From left to right: T. Koyama, T. Sato, R. Morimoto, M. Koyama, T. Kato, T. Kaminoda, H. Friman, C. Gilmore, C. Warren, and M. Yamaguchi. *Photo by T. Joko and courtesy of T. Kaminoda.*

A few months later, on October 22, 1998, a visiting delegation of eight martial artists came to Milwaukee from Japan to pay their respects. Led by Kaminoda Sensei, the group performed a brief, formal service at the grave site. The interstate traffic rushing by that afternoon passed through clouds of incense wafting over the fence. Did people catch a brief glimpse of a small group of Japanese and Americans kneeling in the midst of a veterans cemetery? Did they see the flash of a burning candle, or the light reflecting from the sake and water bottles placed on the grave? I wonder what they said to friends and family that evening about their journey home.

index

Abe, Ichiro, 13
Alexander, Howard, 13
Armstrong, Hunter, 20, 31, 33
Asian Fighting Arts, 7, 21
Broadbent, Art, 2
Bluming, Jon, 4-5, 10, 16
Book of the Sword, 11
Bregman, Jim, 5-6
Burton, Richard F., 2, 11-12, 29
Chicago Judo Club, 2
Classical Budo, 25
Classical Bujutsu, 25, 29
Comprehensive Asian Fighting Arts, 7
Detroit Judo Club, 3
Enoeda, Keinnosuke, 8
Fuller, Bill, 5
Geesink, Anton, 14
A Book of Five Rings (Gorin no sho), 22-24
Hall, David A., 32
Inokuma, Isao, 5, 7
International Hoplological Research Center, 1, 28, 31
International Hoplology Society, 31
Ishikawa, Takehiko, 3
Ito, Kazuo, 27
Iwo Jima, 28
jo (short staff), 1, 12-13, 15, 17, 28, 36
jojutsu (stick fighting), 17, 28
jujutsu, 21, 23, 27
jukendo (the art of the bayonet), 27
Kaminoda, Tsunemori, 4, 35-37
Kano, Jigoro, 27
kenjutsu, 13, 36
Kodokan, 1, 6, 13, 27
Lineberger, Pat, 18-19

Martial Arts International, 4
Mifune, Kyuzo, 27
Miyamoto, Musashi, 21-24
Modern Bujutsu and Budo, 25
Nurse, Paul, 7
O'Neill, Pat, 4
Osako, Johnny, 2-3
Pentagon Dojo, 3
Pentjak Silat, 13
Otake, Risuke, 7, 12-13, 15
Rogers, Doug, 5, 7
Sato, Shizuya, 27
Sentiment of the Sword, 11
Shimizu, Takaji, 4, 16, 36
Shindo Muso-ryu, 16-17, 19, 25, 27, 36
Shinkage-ryu, 22
Society for the Promotion of Ancient Japanese Martial Arts and Ways, 28
Strength and Health magazine, 3
taijiquan, 4, 17-18
Tenshin Shoden Katori Shito-ryu, 6, 12, 23, 27
Tripier Army Medical Center, 18-19
Tuttle Publishing, 9
U.S. Jodo Federation, 1
U.S. Judo Black Belt Federation, 1, 27
U.S. Marine Corps, 4, 8, 27
University of Hawaii, 7, 18, 29, 33
weight-lifting, 1, 3, 5, 16
Wang, Shuchin, 4, 14
Wood National Cemetery, 35-36
yakuza, 4-5
You Only Live Twice, 7, 26
xingyiquan, 4
Zheng Manqing, 14, 17

www.ingramcontent.com/pod-product-compliance
Lightning Source LLC
Chambersburg PA
CBHW071040080526
44587CB00015B/2701